BEI GRIN MACHT SICH IHR WISSEN BEZAHLT

- Wir veröffentlichen Ihre Hausarbeit, Bachelor- und Masterarbeit

- Ihr eigenes eBook und Buch - weltweit in allen wichtigen Shops

- Verdienen Sie an jedem Verkauf

Jetzt bei www.GRIN.com hochladen und kostenlos publizieren

Bal Patil

The Jaina and the British

Bal Patil speech: Tübingen University International Jain Workshop 19. & 20. Feb. 2010

GRIN Verlag

Bibliografische Information der Deutschen Nationalbibliothek:

Die Deutsche Bibliothek verzeichnet diese Publikation in der Deutschen National-
bibliografie; detaillierte bibliografische Daten sind im Internet über http://dnb.d-
nb.de/ abrufbar.

Impressum:

Copyright © 2010 GRIN Verlag, Open Publishing GmbH
Druck und Bindung: Books on Demand GmbH, Norderstedt Germany
ISBN: 978-3-640-71330-1

Dieses Buch bei GRIN:

http://www.grin.com/de/e-book/157283/the-jaina-and-the-british

GRIN - Your knowledge has value

Der GRIN Verlag publiziert seit 1998 wissenschaftliche Arbeiten von Studenten, Hochschullehrern und anderen Akademikern als eBook und gedrucktes Buch. Die Verlagswebsite www.grin.com ist die ideale Plattform zur Veröffentlichung von Hausarbeiten, Abschlussarbeiten, wissenschaftlichen Aufsätzen, Dissertationen und Fachbüchern.

Besuchen Sie uns im Internet:

http://www.grin.com/

http://www.facebook.com/grincom

http://www.twitter.com/grin_com

At the outset I extend my grateful thanks to the very kind invitation extended
by Dr.Andrea Luithle-Hardenberg and her very concerned efforts to persuade me
to attend this distinguished International Tuebingen Workshop on a very
important topic The Jaina and the British. However I would not be able to make
the trip to the University of Tuebingen to participate in this important Conference
as   medically advised. Therefore, I extend my heartfelt apologies to the
organizers of the workshop. I have great pleasure in extending my greetings to
the distinguished scholars participating in this Conference.

I took German as a second language almost as an intuitive choice. Little did I
know that I would be having an opportunity to translate Dr.Alsdorf's book asked
by my mentor in Jain studies, Dr.A.N. Upadhye a great Prakrit Jain   scholar   a
former President of the *All-India Oriental Conference* and also General Editor of
the renowned Bharatiya Jnana Pitha publications. *Moortidevi Jain grandthmala*

It has launched me on a German voyage of Indology-not an indologist
myself- but translator of eminent Indological authors such as Ludwig Alsdorf,
and Colette Caillat,(I translated from French her *Le Jinisme*, published as *Jainism*
(Macmillan,1974) which brings me to this Tuebingen Seminar! I read Albert
Schweitzer's *My Life and Thought* and was much impressed by his book *Indian
Thought and Its Development*, and particularly his observation on the pioneering
role of Jain *ahimsa* in human history.

I am proud to state that My translation of Dr. Ludwig. Alsdorf's German
Beitraege zur Geschichte von Vegetarismus und Rinderverehrung in Indien
(History of Vegetarianism and Cow Veneration In India) has been published
(Routledge, London) in Feb.2010 edited by Dr. Bollee

Dr. Schweitzer speaks in glowing terms of the principle of *Ahimsa* non-
violence as laid down by Jainism: "The laying down of the commandment not to
kill and not to damage is one of the greatest events in the spiritual history of
mankind. Starting from its principle, founded on world and life denial of
abstention from action, ancient Indian thought and this is a period when in other
respects ethics have not progressed very far reaches the tremendous discovery
that ethics know no bounds. So far as we know this is for the first time clearly
expressed by Jainism."

The principle of *ahimsa* (non-violence) and the prescription of strict
vegetarianism are the prime and unique characteristics of Jain religion and ethics.
That the concept of *ahimsa* was foreign to *Vedic* culture is shown by the eminent
Indologist Prof. W. Norman Brown in his *Tagore Memorial Lectures*, 1964-65,
Man in the Universe:

"Though the Upanishads contain the first literary reference to the idea of
rebirth and to the notion that one's action-karma determines the conditions of
one's future existences, and though they arrive at the point of recognising that
rebirth may occur not only in animal form but also in animal bodies, they tell us
nothing about the precept of *ahimsa*. Yet that precept is later associated with the

belief that a soul in its wandering may inhabit both kinds of forms. Ancient Brahmanical literature is conspicuously silent about *ahimsa*. The early Vedic texts do not even record the noun *ahimsa* nor know the ethical meaning which the noun later designated... Nor is an explanation of *ahimsa* deducible from other parts of *Vedic* literature. The ethical concept which it emdodies was entirely foreign to the thinking of the early *Vedic Aryans*, who recognised no kinship between human and animal creation, but rather ate meat and offered animals the sacrifice to the gods." (pp.53-54)

Therefore Prof. Brown concludes: "The double doctrine of *ahimsa* and vegetarianism has never had full and unchallenged acceptance and practice among Hindus, and should not be considered to have arisen in Brahmanical circles. It seems more probable that it originated in non-Brahmanical environment, and was promoted in historic India by the Jains and adopted by Brahmanic Hinduism."

I propose to discuss Jain minority issue as it has evolved in the last hundred years. The remarkable thing about the Jain minority issue is that it was duly noted by the contemporary British rulers as far back as in 1909. Even more significantly the Census of India has been counting the Jains as a separate religious community right from the first census in 1873. With the dawn of the Indian freedom the Jain community did present its claim for minority status to the Constituent Assembly during the formation of the Indian Constitution.

It would be also most relevant to refer here to the two one anna coins minted during the East India Company regime in 1818 depicting Bhagwan Mahavira and Bhagvan Parsvanatha.

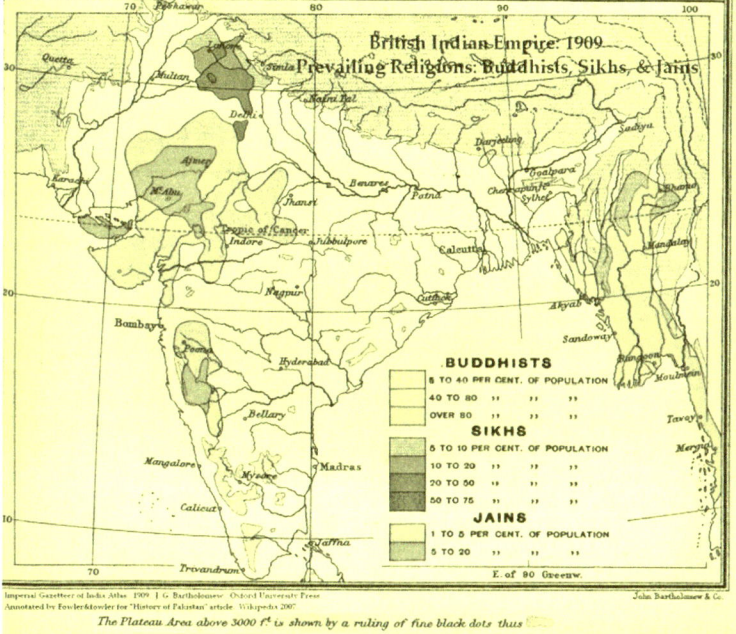

Then I would like to refer to the *Imperial Gazeteer* showing the British Indian Empire map in 1909 in which prevailing religions are shown as Buddhists, Sikhs and Jains. This I think as a most remarkable acknowledgment by the British India of Jainism as a distinct religious entity in India.

Yet the Jain leaders continued their efforts and made several representations to the non-statutory *National Commission for Minorities* for their designation as a national minority. Later with the enactment of *National Commission for Minorities Act* in 1992 Muslims, Christians, Sikhs, Buddhists and Zoroastrians (Parsis) were notified as minorities omitting inexplicably the Jains. But due to their persistent representations finally the NCM recommended for the inclusion of the Jain community but it was not notified thus by the Government.

The entire constitutional, legal and political process of the recognition of the Jain minority status is rendered confusion worse confounded by the interpretative *'Hindutva'* parameters whether, political, religious and judicial-particularly as evidenced in the latest Supreme Court judgement in my Petition *(Bal Patil & anr Vs. Union of India)* which has in its *obiter dicta* stated that the "Hinduism is the common faith of India" and "Jainism is a special religion".

As an extreme example I can cite the case of my complaint against the Editor, *The Hindu*-a prominent Indian daily- re: a report as follows:

"The Central Government's reported move to give Scheduled Caste status to Dalit Christians and Dalit Muslims will deprive current SCs (among the Hindus, Sikhs, Jains and Buddhists) of their job and education quotas, according to Vijay Sonkar, President of *All India Scheduled Caste Reservation Protection Forum*." Despite my complaint to the Press Council of India and the Press Council's direction to *The Hindu* Editor *The Hindu* has not yet published my rejoinder.

Another example relates to misrepresentation of Jain Digambar community by Mr Soli Sorabjee, the former Attorney General of India, and an eminent jurist. He has tendered apology in a civil suit of defamation filed by me for having defamed the Jain Digambar religious community through comments in a column in an English daily in Mumbai in 2003. Mr.Soli Sorabjee had written in his *"Out of Court"* column in *Times of India* that "The urge to bare one's body springs from different compulsions. a certain sect of Jains- Digambars- who move about uncovered in public invoke their right of religious freedom."

As the concerned English daily failed to publish a rejoinder objecting to its defamatory implications and as there was no response even after a complaint was lodged with the Press Council of India I filed a defamation suit in the City Civil Court. In the recent hearing on the matter it was pleaded on behalf of Mr.Sorabjee that when writing the impugned observations he had no intention to hurt or insult the religious susceptibilities of the Digambar Jain religious community, and if inadvertantly it has caused any hurt he regrets the same. Satisfied with this expression of regret I withdrew the defamation proceedings against Mr.Sorabjee, but defamations proceedings against the concerned English paper, its publishers, and the editor continue.

I am always puzzled why most historians, commentators, when they begin their search start with the phrase: 'Jainism like Buddhism..., I cannot make out why nobody ever begins with the phrase :'Buddhism like Jainism..., Sometimes I wonder, forgive my impertinence, if there is an unwritten conspiracy to somehow bury Jainism in the historical fossils as if it is a relic of some forgotten credo of no consequence in the history of religions.

Apart from a few exceptions, most histories and encyclopaedias of world religions fail to mention Jainism as an independent religion. There are pervasive misconceptions about the origin of Jainism, about its relation to Vedic-Brahmanic Hinduism, about Mahavira being the founder of Jainism, about Jainism being an offshoot of Buddhism or Hinduism, or a reformist sect of Hinduism. There are misrepresentations galore. Jainism is overshadowed by Hinduism and Buddhism and, if noticed at all, is mentioned in passing as one of the ancient Indian religious movements subsidary to Buddhism.

Almost all the scholars agree that Jainism has pre-Aryan roots in the religious and cultural history of India. As Dr. A. N. Upadhye remarked – "The origins of Jainism go back to the pre-historic times. They are to be sought in the fertile valley of Ganga, where they flourished in the past, even before the advent of Aryans with their priestly religion, a society of recluses who laid much stress on individual exertion, on practice of a code of morality and devotion to austerities, as means of attaining religious Summum Bonum." (*Jainism* by Colette Caillat, A.N. Upadhye & Bal Patil, Macmillan, 1974)

In fact, the Jain system of thought is so wonderfully consistent with modern realism and science that one may easily be tempted to question its antiquity, about which, however, there is now no doubt. as Dr. Walthur Schubring observes, "He who has a thorough knowledge of the structure of the world cannot but admire the inward logic and harmony of Jain ideas. Hand in hand with the refined cosmographical ideas goes a high standard of astronomy and mathematics." Dr. Hermann Jacobi also believes that "Jainism goes back to a very early period, and to primitive currents of religious and metaphysical speculation, which gave rise to the oldest Indian philosophies. They (the Jains) seem to have worked out their system from the most primitive notions about matter."

In the Buddhist scripture *Majjima Nikaya*, Buddha himself tells us about his ascetic life and its ordinances which are in conformity with the Jain monk's code of conduct. He says, "Thus far, *SariPutta*, did I go in my penance. I went without clothes. I licked my food from my hands. I took no food that was brought or meant especially for me. I accepted no invitation to a meal." Mrs. Rhys Davis has observed that Buddha found his two teachers Alara and Uddaka at Vaisali and started his religious life as a Jain.

Such is the context of the pervasive impact of the misleading Indian historiography from the deleterious effects of which even the most eminent historians, both right and left are not immune. One of the consequences of this failure is the continuing hold of misleading stereotypes of the nature of Indic religious thought and practice. I think this has a vital bearing on the devastatingly damaging impact of the misconceived Indological and 'Oriental' stereotypes on the Indian ethno-religious historiography so as to necessitate a paradigmatic revaluation.

This misinterpretation of history is compounded by what the doyen of Indian Indologists, Dr.R.G. Bhandarkar noted as to how "India has no written history. Nothing was known till within recent times of the political condition of the country, the dynasties that ruled over the different provisions which composed it, and the great religious and social revolutions it went through. The historical curiosity of the people was satiated by legends. What we find of a historical nature in the literature of the country before the arrival of the Mahomedans comes to very little." P. i-ii (*Early History of the Dekkan Down to the Mahomedan Conquest,* 2nd Ed. 1983)

Such is the common strategy of the historians, philosophers and academicians in dealing with the Indic *Sramanic* religious traditions. Issues are obscured, by introducing irrelevancies and thus an attitude of contemptuous prejudice is provoked by exciting ridicule.

The Jain demand for minority status is now a century old. When in British India the Viceroy took a decision in principle that the Government would give representation to *"Important Minorities"* in the Legislative Council, (Petition dt.2nd September,1909,) Seth Manekchand Hirachand, acting President of *Bharatvarshiya Digambar Jain Mahasabha*, thus appealed to the Viceroy and Governor-General of India, Lord Minto, for the inclusion of the Jain community as an *Important Minority*. The Viceroy responded positively to this petition informing that in giving representation to minorities by nomination the claim of the important Jain community will receive full consideration'. Seth Maneckchand's Petition was transferred to the Government of Bombay and the Secretary to the Govt. of Bombay stated in his reply dt.15th October, 1909.[2]

"I am directed to inform you that a number of seats have been reserved for the representation of minorities by nominated and that in allotting them the claim of the important Jain Community will receive full consideration."

The National Commission for Minorities Act, 1992 does not make any reference to religious minority community but defines minority for the purpose of the Act to mean a community notified as such by the Central Government', whereas, in one way or the other, Jain community has been declared as a religious minority by the various High Courts and by the State Governments pursuant to the definition given in the State's Act or other wise.

It may be mentioned that the Jain community has been declared as minority religious community under the various state enactments by invoking their authority under Art. 30 of the Constitution of India. But under the provision of the *National Commission for Minorities Act, 1992*, Muslims, Christians, Sikhs, Buddhists and Zoroastrians have been declared which lays down that minority for the purpose of the Act of 1992 means a community notified as such by the central government. There are no guide lines for such declaration. The Jain community has already been declared a minority religious community in Karnataka, M.P., U.P., Jharkhand, West Bengal, Rajasthan, Uttaranchal, Maharashtra and Delhi. In Calcutta, Delhi, Mumbai and Madras Jains have been recognized as a minority by the respective High Courts of that State. In other part of the country condition of the Jains is the same. Thus there is proper identification on a State basis.

At the dawn of the Indian freedom the President of the Constituent Assembly Dr. Rajendra Prasad had nominated Mr. Kasturbhai Lalbhai, a Jain industrialist as a Jain representative to Minority Advisory Committee to the Constituent Assembly.

Sardar Patel in his letter of 25th August 1946 addressed to Sir Bhagchandji Soni, *President, All India Digamber Jain Mahasabha* assured the Jain community that "in free India there would be no restrictions upon the religious liberty of any community and there need be no apprehensions in this regard"

On 25th January, 1950, a Jain delegation was led to the Prime Minister Jawaharlal Nehru and other central leaders to draw their attention to the anomalous position of the Jains under *sub-clause (b) of Clause 2* of *Article 25* and a petition was submitted. Jawaharlal Nehru clearly assured the delegation that the Jains are not Hindus and on 31-1-1950, his Principal Private Secretary, Mr.A.V. Pai wrote the following letter:

"This Article merely makes a definition. This definition by enforcing a specific consitutional arrangement circumscribes that rule. Likewise you will note that this mentions not only Jains but also Buddhists and Sikhs. It is clear that Buddhists are not Hindus and therefore there need be no apprehension that the Jains are designated as Hindus. There is no doubt that the Jains are a different religious community and this accepted position is in no way affected by the Constitution."

No: 33/94/50-PMS.

PRIME MINISTER'S SECRETARIAT
NEW DELHI

31st January, 1950.

Dear Sir,

With reference to the deputation of certain representatives of the Jains, who met the Prime Minister on the 25th January, I am desired to say that there is no cause whatever for the Jains to have any apprehensions regarding the future of their religion and community. Your deputation drew attention to Article 25, Explanation II, of the Constitution. This Explanation only lays down a rule of construction for the limited purposes of one provision in the Article, and, as you will notice, it mentions not only Jains, but also the Buddhists and the Sikhs. It is clear that Buddhists are not Hindus. Therefore, there is no reason for thinking that Jains are considered as Hindus. It is true that Jains are in some ways closely allied to Hindus and have many customs in common; but there can be no doubt that they are a distinct religious community and the Constitution does not in any way affect this well-recognised position.

Yours faithfully,

A.V.Pai

(A.V.Pai).
Principal Private Secretary
to the Prime Minister.

Shri S.G.Patil,
Representative of Jains Deputation,
10, Central Court, New Delhi.

It is also a matter of pride for the Jain community that the official Indian Constitution copy in the *Lok Sabha*- Parliament of India- includes the following picture of Mahavira's message of *Ahimsa*:

Vardhamana Mahavir, the 24th Tirthankara in a meditative posture, another illustration from the Calligraphed edition of the Constitution of India. Jainism is another stream of spiritual renaissance which seeks to refine and sublimate man's conduct and emphasises Ahimsa, non violence, as the means to achieve it. This became a potent weapon in the hands of Mahatma Gandhi in his political struggle against the British Empire.

भारतीय संविधान में प्रकाशित

हिन्दी अनुवाद

चौबीसवें तीर्थंकर वर्धमान महावीर ध्यान-मुद्रा में, भारतीय संविधान के लिखित संस्करण से। जैनधर्म आध्यात्मिक क्रान्ति की वह धारा है जो मनुष्य के चारित्र को परिष्कृत/उदात्त करने की दिशा में सक्रिय है। यह धारा अहिंसा पर जोर देती है और इसे उदात्त चारित्र की प्राप्ति का साधन मानती है। ब्रिटिश-साम्राज्य के विरुद्ध राजनैतिक संघर्ष में अहिंसा महात्मा गांधी के हाथों में एक शक्तिशाली हथियार सिद्ध हुआ।

It is, however, pertinent to note in this context the insidious impact of the Hinduisation process on the Jaina population. Hinduism has never been a proselytizing religion like Christianity and Islam but the way the *Hindutva* propaganda is operating that Jains are Hindus the result is a surreptious conversion of Jains by their misleading enumeration as Hindus in the census. This is glaringly evident in the Census figures.

Ever since I became involved with the question of the Jain religious community as a minority I have not ceased to wonder what it is in Jainism that makes the Hindutva fundamentalists who are determined to absorb Jainism into its labyrinthine bosom , and other innocent fellow-travellers to make Jains part and parcel of their hybrid melange of diverse religious beliefs and practices. This peculiar acquisitive trend is not only confined to the well-defined agenda of the champions of *'Hindu Rashtra'* or the Hindu nation conceived as such by Sawarkar *"Asindhu Sindhu Paryanta yasya Bharatbhumika pitrubhu punyabhu sarvaih hindu iti smritah*" i.e. "One who considers the country or nation spread between the Sindhu river and the sea as his Fatherland and Holy Land is verily a Hindu."-the godfather of the concept of Hindutva but also their fellow-travellers.

How did this modern myth of Hinduism begin? It had its origin in the Orientalism created by the colonial Sanskrit scholars in the 19th century. As Richard King has discussed in his book *Orientalism and Religion :Postcolonial Theory, India and The Mystic East'*

As he notes succinctly regarding the Constitutional clubbing of the Buddhists,Jains and Sikhs in *Article 25 Expl.II* which he thinks unacceptable because:

"First, it rides roughshod over religious diversity and established group-affiliations. Second, such an approach ignores the non-Brahmanical and non-Vedic elements of these traditions...In the last analysis, neo-Vedantic inclusivism remains inappropriate for the simple reason that Buddhists and Jains do not generally see themselves as followers of sectarian denominationsof 'Hinduism'." (pp108-09)

This colonial construction of 'Hinduism' contributed according to Richard King to the merging of the Brahmanical forms of religion with Hinduism which is notable in the "tendency to emphasize Vedic and brahmanical texts and beliefs as central and foundational to the 'essence of Hinduism and in the modern association of 'Hindu doctrine' with the various brahmanical schools of the Vedanta..."p.102

The historiographical ambiguity and the confusion worse confounded caused by such orientation caused is well documented in Prof D.N. Jha's address to the 66th session of the Indian History Congress as its General President: *Looking for a Hindu Identity* (*http://www.sacw.net/India_History/dnj_Jan06.pdf.*)

The 8 August, 2005 Judgment of the 3 Judges Bench of the Supreme Court consisting of Chief Justice R. C. Lahoti, Justice D. M. Dharmadhikari and Justice P. K. Balasubramanyan, in the *Bal Patil Case (CA 4730 of 1999)*, written by Justice Dharmadhikari has not only declined to act on the recommendation of the National Commission for Minorities for the declaration of Jain community as a religious minority community on par with Muslim, Christian, Sikh, Buddhist and Zoroastrian (Parsi) but also its *obiter dicta* place Hindu religion above all other religions.

The Supreme Court bases its rejection of the Jaina claim for minority status on the 11 Judges Bench decision in the *T.M.A. Pai Case [2002(8) SSC 481]* which was related to the scope of Article 30 of the Constitution on the right of a linguistic, religious or cultural minority to establish and administer educational institutions of its choice.

In the judgment, the Supreme Court opined: "Thus, 'Hinduism' can be called a general religion and common faith of India whereas 'Jainism' is a special religion formed on the basis of quintessence of Hindu religion."

As noted by Syed Shahabuddin (IFS (Retd.), Ex-MP, Supreme Court Advocate, *President, AIMMM*) in his article commenting on this judgement published in the *Milli Gazette Nov.3, 2005* and *The Tribune, Nov.25, 2005* :

"His historiography is full of flaws...All constitutional safeguards and assurances under the Constitution and in international law shall be reduced to zero if the distinct identity of any religious group, howsoever small, is denied and any group is forced to relate to Hinduism as a sect or sub-sect. The Sikhs and the Jains and the Buddhists will not accept Hindu hegemony on the ground that they are all branches of the same tree, which has sprung from the same soil. Dharmadhikari J.'s views clearly reflect the Hindutva philosophy. It is time that the Supreme Court frees itself of any lurking intellectual subservience to the Hindutva philosophy."

However, the late eminent jurist L.M. Singhvi, the *Founder President of the World Jain Confederation*, has observed: "The judgment in *Bal Patil case* is a judgment of three judges which goes against the judgment of 11 judges and many previous judgments of larger benches on the basis of which Jains must be recognised as a distinct religious minority, distinct and separate from the Hindus. Indeed, inclusive reference to Jains and Sikhs in *Article 25* of the Constitution clearly indicates that Jains, Sikhs and Buddhists despite being separate and distinct were accepted as minority religions. Pt.Jawaharlal Nehru himself clarified many a times that Jains are an ancient minority. They have been recognized as a minority by notifications in Maharashtra, Uttar Pradesh and Madhya Pradesh."

The real issue now is declaration of national minority status for the Jain religious community in India. Jains have been declared a minority in Maharashtra, Karnataka, Madhya Pradesh, Uttar Pradesh, Rajasthan, Delhi, West Bengal, Uttaranchala and Jharkhand States . The total population of the Jain minority declared minority thus comes to 3,678, 551. The total Jain population in India is 4,225, 053. Thus the percentage of the Jain minority population comes to 88%. Yet being less than 50% to constitute a minority population in the whole of India is no longer taken into account.

The question is : Are all the benefits only meant for the national minorities so-called? I do not mean any disrespect to the national minorities so designated under the National Minorities Commission act. But I am constrained to take a strong exception to the blatantly discriminatory manner in which the Jains declared as a minority in various States such as Maharashtra, Karnataka, Madhya Pradesh, Uttar Pradesh, Delhi, West Bengal, Uttaranchala, Chhattisgarh, Jharkhand, Rajasthan comprising 88% of the total Jain population in India the Jain minority students in these States are specifically excluded from the benefit of the Pre and Post-Matriculation Scholarships announced under the *Prime Minister's 15-Point Plan* in co-operation with similar State Government packages because Jains are not a National Minority!!. I am constrained to state that this smacks of being Jain Apartheid.

A meeting of the Union Cabinet, chaired by Prime Minister Manmohan Singh, on 19th December, 2008   approved a proposal to introduce the *Constitution 103rd Amendment Bill* to define minority. " This Bill is about the power to define a minority. The Supreme Court directed the Centre to decide the issue of giving minority status to Jains in *Bal Patil vs. Union of India* in 2005. A number of orders have been passed by the Supreme Court in this behalf," Home Minister, P.Chidambaram said.

It is inconceivable however that this amendment will be passed in the Indian Parliament because the main national minorities, Muslim, Christian and Sikh are not willing to arrive at a definition of minority status on the basis of State population because Sikhs are a majority in Punjab State as recently ruled by the Supreme Court of India and Christians are a majority in North-Eastern States Mizoram, Meghalaya and Muslims are a majority in Jammu & Kashmir. Besides the passage of this Bill will require two-thirds majority.

Thus Jains, Budddhists and Zoroastrians (Parsis) remain the national religious minorities in the real sense of the term''

Irrespective of any other test the Government of India and the Minority Affairs Ministry in co-operation with the National commission for Minorities should have followed the following Indian Army signpost in the Himalayas which is so utterly secular in character:

Thus Jain minority matter has reached a decisive stage testing whether the Government of India has the courage to distinguish the real constitutional and demographic religious minorities from the ones declared already.

13

I give below urls to a few of my articles on Jainism and related issues:

http://www.youtube.com/watch?v=m4qqI_VO0fc

- THE JAINA AND THE BRITISH: JAIN MINORITY [4/4]
- THE JAINA AND THE BRITISH: JAIN MINORITY [3/4]
- THE JAINA AND THE BRITISH: JAIN MINORITY [2/4]
- THE JAINA AND THE BRITISH: JAIN MINORITY [1/4]

The History of Vegetarianism and Cow-Veneration in India
By Ludwig Alsdorf, Translated by **Bal Patil**. Edited by Willem Bollee. Series: Routledge Advances in Jaina Studies. List Price: $135.00 ...

http://www.uni-tuebingen.de//uni/aid/Jaina%20WS.pdf

14

Bal Patil
http://www.facebook.com/note.php?saved&&suggest&note_id=308
098959505#!/bal.patil?ref=profile

Articles:

The Rise, Decline And Renewals Of Sramanic Religious Traditions Within Indic
Civilisation
With Particular Reference To The Evolution Of Jain Sramanic Culture
And Its Impact On The Indic Civilization

**(A Paper presented in the Conference on Religions in Indic Civilisation in New Delhi,
December, 18-21, 2003, Organised by the Centre for theStudy of Developing Societies in
collaboration with International Association for the History of Religions and India
International Centre.)**

- The Rise, Decline And Renewals Of Sramanic Religious Traditions Within Indic Civilisation
  With Particular Reference To The Evolution Of Jain Sramanic Culture And Its Impact On The Indic
  Civilization
- Dr. L.M. Singhvi - A Tribute
- Jain Religious Minority Status - Update
- UN General Assembly Resolution Declaring Mahatma Gandhi Birthday, 2nd October, as International
  Day of Non-Violence
- Dr. Albert Schweitzer The Saint of Lambarene
- The Great Ahmedabad Trial Of Mahatma Gandhi 1922
- http://www.countercurrents.org/hr-patil271106.htm
- Is Jain Minority Right In India Receiving A Fair Deal? By Bal Patil
-
- ## Assault on Jainism
  The Gujarat Freedom of Religion (Amendment) Bill 2006: Jains and Buddhists as
  Hindus
- http://sabrang.com/cc/archive/2006/dec06/forum.html

Gujarat State Freedom of Religion Bill

http://en.wikipedia.org/wiki/Legal_status_of_Jainism_as_a_distinct_religion_in_In
dia

Bal Patil & Anr. v. Union of India & Ors. **Supreme Court Decided on 08/08/2005**

Indian Supreme Court Judgement Obiter Dicta Places Hindu Religion Above All Religions

History of Vegetarianism and Cow-Veneration | Indologica
BAL PATIL is an independent researcher, journalist and Chairman of the **Jain** Minority Status
Committee, Dakshin Bharat **Jain** Sabha, a century old **Jain** ...